MAGIC SPELLS
Coloring book

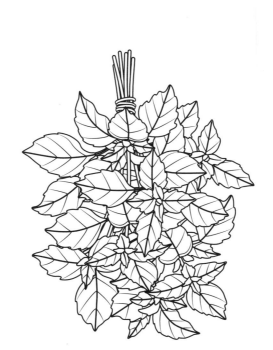

MAGIC SPELLS
Coloring book

SIRIUS

This edition published in 2023 by Sirius Publishing, a division of
Arcturus Publishing Limited,
26/27 Bickels Yard, 151–153 Bermondsey Street,
London SE1 3HA

ISBN: 978-1-3988-3018-9
CH011163NT

Printed in China

Introduction

Magic has been around for as long as humans have. Even to this day symbols are seen and used across the world, from the all-seeing eye to pentagrams. Many active covens exist today, and the occult and magic have always intrigued people. This coloring book contains a multitude of illustrations to try out and color in. It includes historical imagery like the cauldron and its keeper Cerridwen, mythical creatures such as Celtic dragons, and practical uses like herbal mixtures that are bundled together for magical intervention. Alongside the images are beneficial spells and information about the magic which existed, and still exists in the world. So, brew yourself a drink, grab your familiar—if you have one—take your colored pencils or pens, and see if you have what it takes to bring these pictures to life!

HOW TO CALL A GRIMALKIN

The grimalkin is a spirit cat of Celtic folklore, possibly inspired by sightings of the Scottish wild-cat. You can call the grimalkin if you are being maligned in any way. Light a grey candle or tealight and say:

Grimalkin, grimalkin uncross my path
Let those who malign me feel your wrath
Ashes to ashes and dust to dust
The past dead and buried, free from mistrust
As I walk my own path, I will have my own say
Grimalkin protect me through each fight and fray

Cerridwen was the keeper of the cauldron of transformation and it is said that Celtic warriors would be taken into her cauldron in death, to be reborn or transformed. In modern magic you can call on Cerridwen to help with any period of change. Write your goal on a slip of paper and burn it in a small cauldron while saying:

Cerridwen, cauldron keeper
Take this desire true
Transform it in your cauldron
Make all that was renew

BLESSING TO FOLLOW YOUR NOSE

This spell is especially fun to use when you're on
holiday or in an unfamiliar place.
Stand for a moment and close your eyes,
then say in your head or out loud:

*Guardians and guides, lead me to a magical place
in this area, one which will bring me joy
and happiness and which will enhance my stay
here in this place. I trust your guidance and
will follow where you lead, knowing that you
keep be safe. Blessed be.
Now, which way should I go?*

Remain standing until you feel a tug or pull
in a certain direction and head that way.

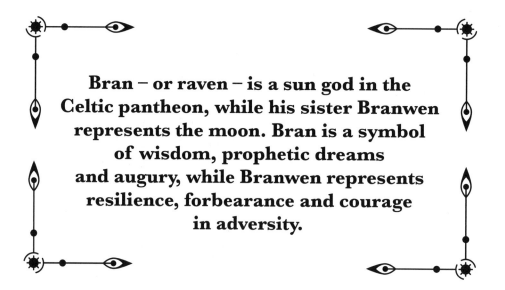

Bran – or raven – is a sun god in the
Celtic pantheon, while his sister Branwen
represents the moon. Bran is a symbol
of wisdom, prophetic dreams
and augury, while Branwen represents
resilience, forbearance and courage
in adversity.

The mandrake is famously associated with witchcraft. Although the roots and leaves are poisonous, the humanoid shape made it perfect to use as a 'poppet' in spell casting. Carrying a mandrake root was said to bring good fortune, though pulling one up by the roots and hearing its scream would cause instant death.

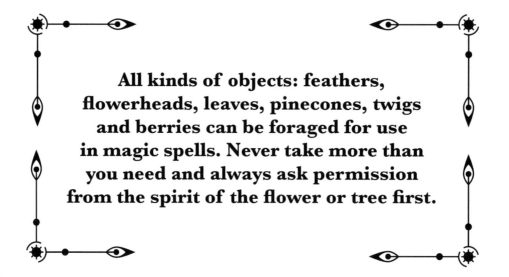

All kinds of objects: feathers,
flowerheads, leaves, pinecones, twigs
and berries can be foraged for use
in magic spells. Never take more than
you need and always ask permission
from the spirit of the flower or tree first.

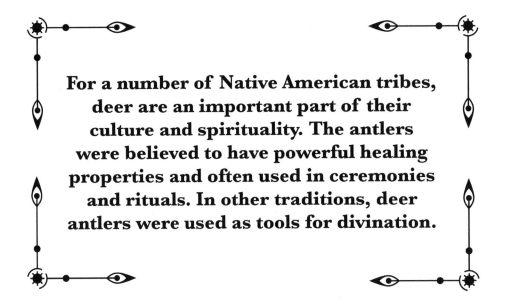

For a number of Native American tribes, deer are an important part of their culture and spirituality. The antlers were believed to have powerful healing properties and often used in ceremonies and rituals. In other traditions, deer antlers were used as tools for divination.

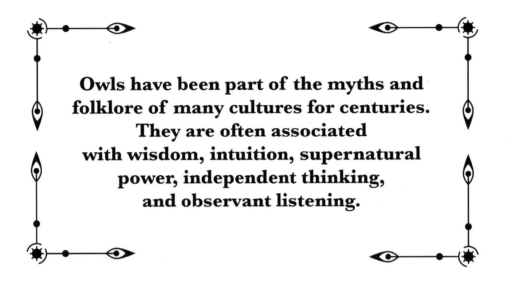

Owls have been part of the myths and
folklore of many cultures for centuries.
They are often associated
with wisdom, intuition, supernatural
power, independent thinking,
and observant listening.

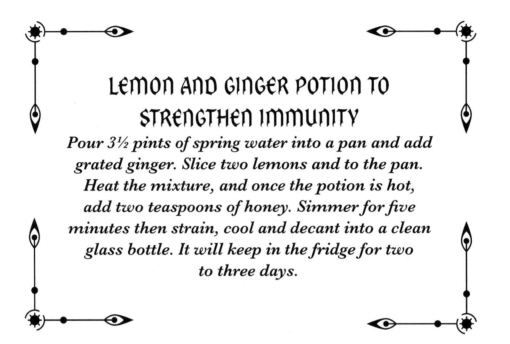

LEMON AND GINGER POTION TO STRENGTHEN IMMUNITY

Pour 3½ pints of spring water into a pan and add grated ginger. Slice two lemons and to the pan. Heat the mixture, and once the potion is hot, add two teaspoons of honey. Simmer for five minutes then strain, cool and decant into a clean glass bottle. It will keep in the fridge for two to three days.

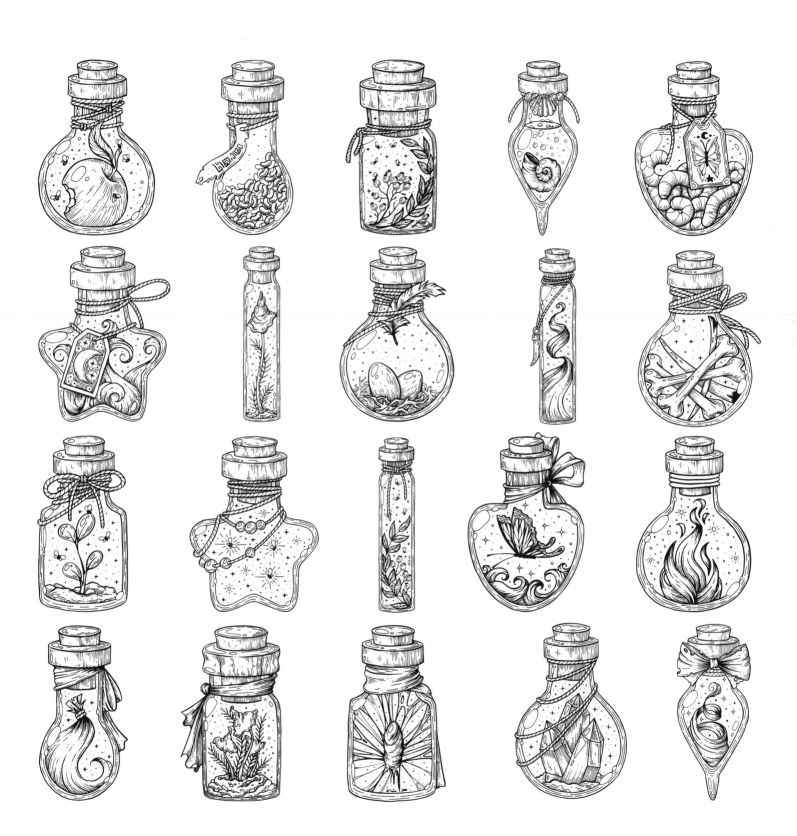

Trees play a very important role in
Celtic magic and in druidry. They have
a number of ways of celebrating
the life of a tree when it is cut down.
These include playing music, bearing
witness to the cutting, raising positive
energy for the tree, and apologizing
to the tree as it is cut.

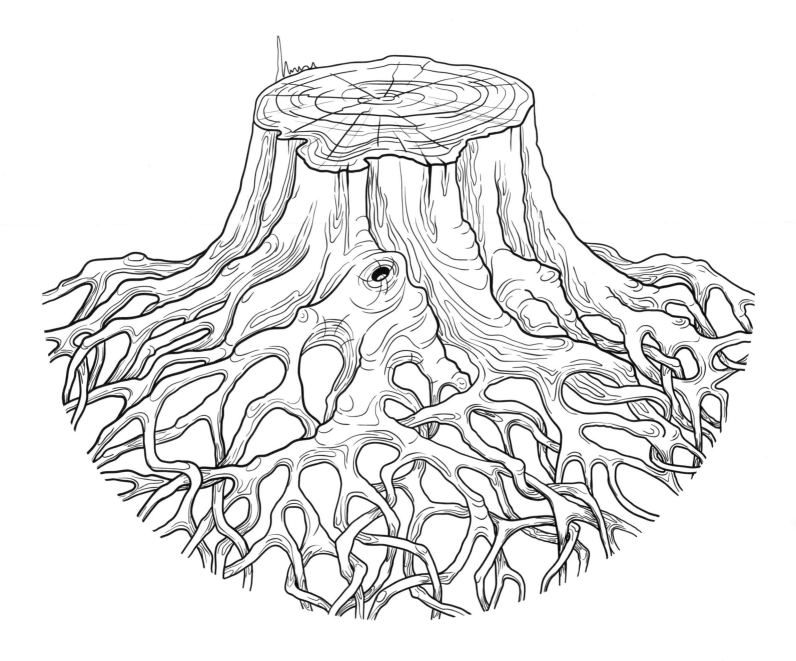

A kelpie is a shape-changing aquatic spirit of Scottish legend. The name may derive from the Scottish Gaelic words 'cailpeach' or 'colpach', which means heifer or colt. Kelpies are said to haunt rivers and streams, usually appearing in the shape of a horse.

Tussie-mussies or nosegays were held
to the nose whenever a bad smell
pervaded the air, allowing the holder to
enjoy the smell of flowers instead.
Make one by gathering fragrant herbs
and flowers into a small, round posy,
tying with a ribbon and cutting the stems
short. Choose blue flowers for healing;
pink for self-love and red for romance.

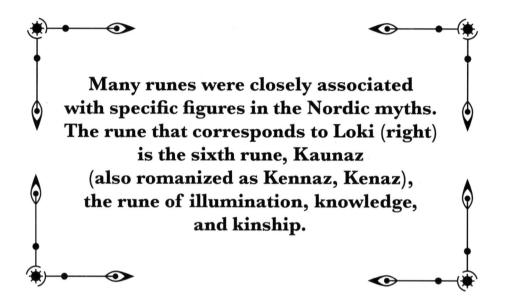

Many runes were closely associated
with specific figures in the Nordic myths.
The rune that corresponds to Loki (right)
is the sixth rune, Kaunaz
(also romanized as Kennaz, Kenaz),
the rune of illumination, knowledge,
and kinship.

The Norse god Odin is associated
with wisdom, healing, death, royalty,
the gallows, knowledge, war, battle,
victory, sorcery, poetry, frenzy, and the
runic alphabet. In later folklore, Odin
sometimes appears as a leader of
the Wild Hunt, a ghostly procession
of the dead through the winter sky.

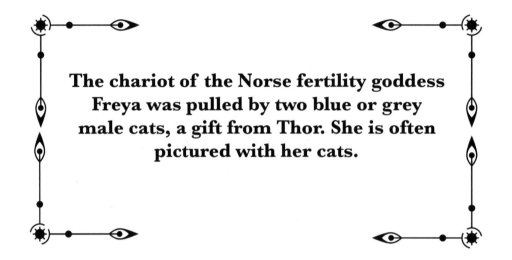

The chariot of the Norse fertility goddess Freya was pulled by two blue or grey male cats, a gift from Thor. She is often pictured with her cats.

Thor, son of Gods, has enhanced longevity, and possesses superhuman strength, speed, agility, durability and immunity to most diseases. His hammer, Mjölnar is used both as an extraordinary weapon and to give blessings.

A pentacle is a round disc with a pentagram or five-pointed star on it. Witches place candles, crystals and other objects on the pentacle to charge them with magical energy. You can make one by drawing a five-pointed star on a plate or disc of modelling clay.

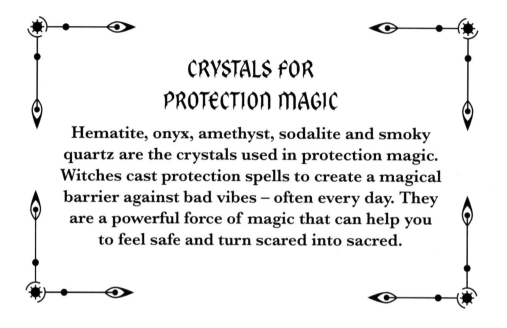

CRYSTALS FOR PROTECTION MAGIC

Hematite, onyx, amethyst, sodalite and smoky quartz are the crystals used in protection magic. Witches cast protection spells to create a magical barrier against bad vibes – often every day. They are a powerful force of magic that can help you to feel safe and turn scared into sacred.

The Celtic ravens, Bran and Branwen are the epitome of family bonds and support, so invoke their aid with this chant if you need to increase your personal support system:

Bran the blessed and Branwen strong
Shape and form my family bonds
Stick together through thick and thin
As a family we will win

In ancient Egypt, cats were considered to be magical creatures, who could bring good luck to those who housed them. They were dressed in jewels and fed delicacies. When Egyptian cats died, they were often mummified. Many have been found in grand tombs, buried alongside the deceased humans.

BLESSING TO PROTECT
DOORS AND WINDOWS

Windows and doors are portals into your home through which negative energies can enter. Use this daily blessing to protect then and prevent harm entering your home. Perform it about a hour before you go to bed. Light a stick of incense and, staring at the main door to your home, use the smoke to draw a pentagram across the door, saying:

Keep safe this house, protected be
None shall cross this boundary
Keep safe this house, a welcome place
To those invited to this space

Move around the house clockwise repeating at every external door and window, then place the incense in a holder to burn out. Repeat daily.

In many ancient cultures the hare represents regeneration, fertility and magic. It was believed that the hare moon was a promise of growth, re-birth, and new beginnings – this is probably related to the hare's associations with high reproductive rates.

WITCH BOTTLE

Fill a small bottle with three pins, three small
nails, three small shards of broken glass and
small crystals of amethyst, hematite and smoky
quartz, then add protective dried herbs and
black salt, white salt, turmeric, garlic powder,
basil, sage, rosemary, foxglove, mugwort and
pine needles. Continue until full and seal the top
with candle wax. Say the following incantation
while holding the bottle in your hands:

Threshold protected
Evil rejected
Doorway guarded
Entrance warded
Wtch bottle hidden
Entry forbidden
All wicked intent
Away it is sent!
Safe from all harm
By witch bottle charms
As I do it
So it shall be.

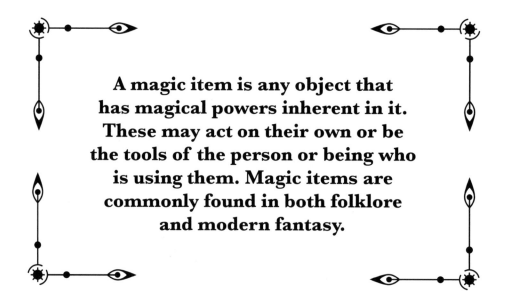

A magic item is any object that
has magical powers inherent in it.
These may act on their own or be
the tools of the person or being who
is using them. Magic items are
commonly found in both folklore
and modern fantasy.

It has been suggested that the link
between witches and brooms or besoms
may come from a pagan fertility ritual,
whereby farmers would dance astride
poles, pitchforks or brooms under
the full moon. They did this to encourage
the growth of their crops. Over the
centuries this 'broomstick dance' became
confused with accounts of witches
flying through the night on their way
to orgies and other illicit meetings.

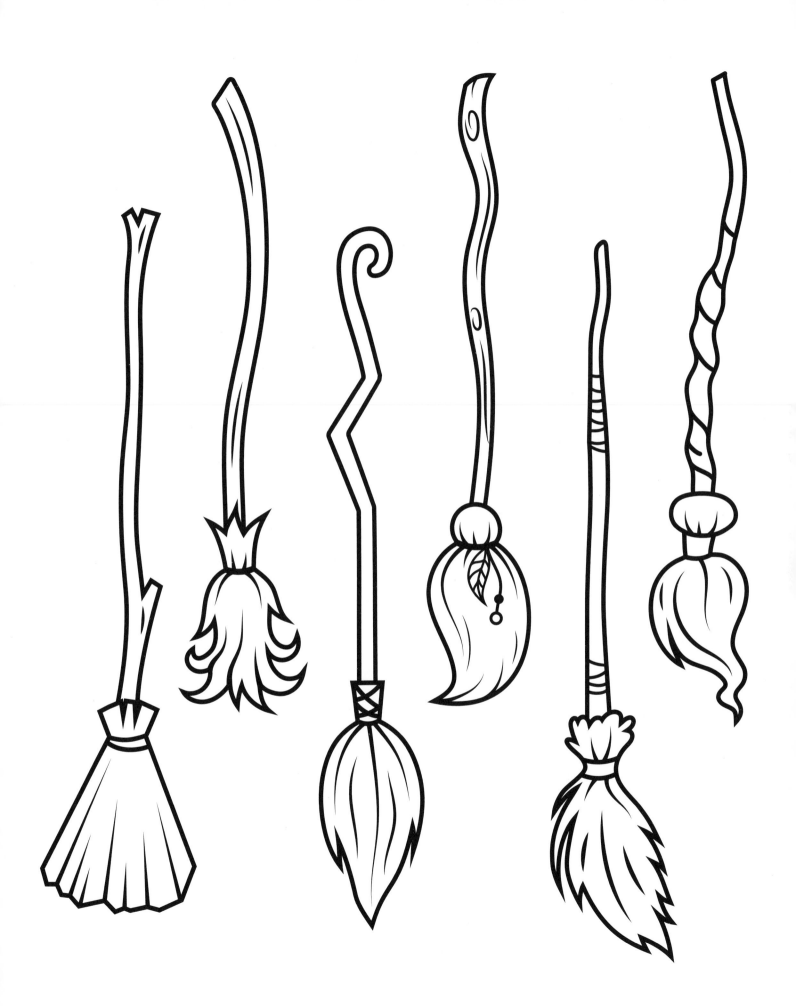

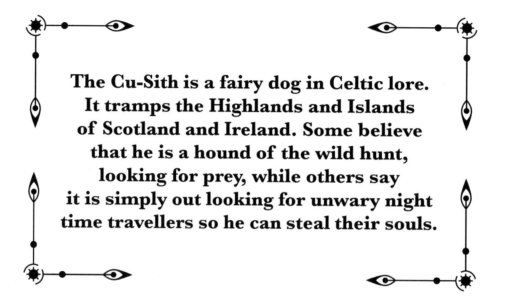

The Cu-Sith is a fairy dog in Celtic lore.
It tramps the Highlands and Islands
of Scotland and Ireland. Some believe
that he is a hound of the wild hunt,
looking for prey, while others say
it is simply out looking for unwary night
time travellers so he can steal their souls.

SPELL TO PROTECT A TREE

Ring out danger, ring out harm
Ring out loud and sound the alarm
When woodsmen come to chop and fell
Their work is thwarted by this spell
Long life to this tree, protected be
Long life to this tree, so shall it be!

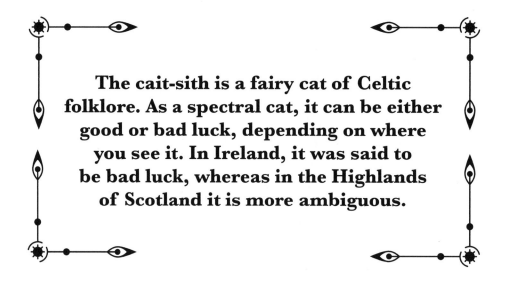

The cait-sith is a fairy cat of Celtic folklore. As a spectral cat, it can be either good or bad luck, depending on where you see it. In Ireland, it was said to be bad luck, whereas in the Highlands of Scotland it is more ambiguous.

According to the Norse sagas, runic inscriptions held magical powers. With the aid of inscriptions, you could predict the future, protect against misfortune, imbue objects with different qualities, or you could write down conjurations, curses and spells.

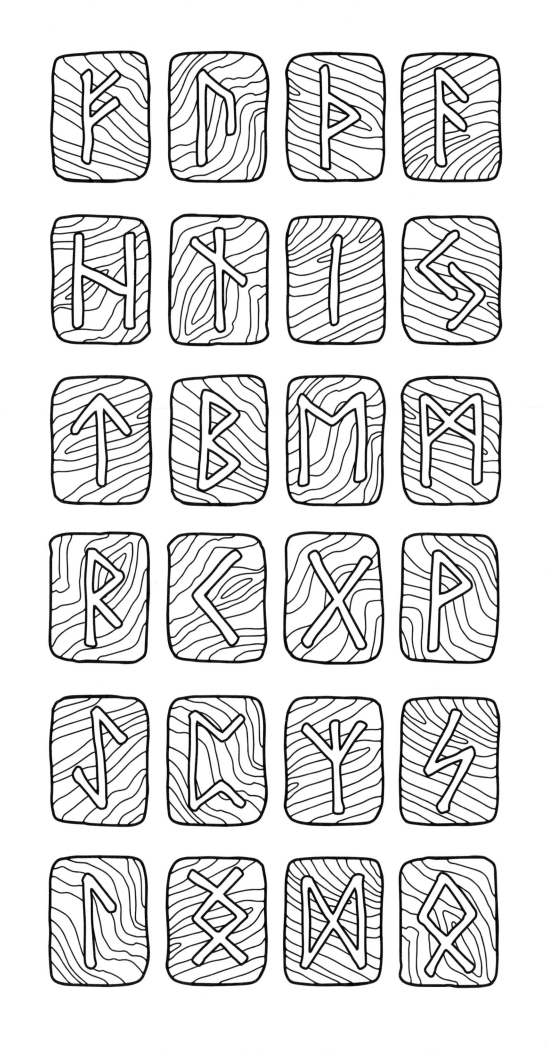

In many African countries,
a large owl hanging around a house
is believed to indicate that a powerful
shaman lives there. Many also believe
that the owl carries messages back
and forth between the shaman and
the spirit world.

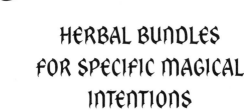

HERBAL BUNDLES
FOR SPECIFIC MAGICAL
INTENTIONS

You can use specific combinations of herbs and
flowers to achieve particular outcomes in magic.
These include:

Cleansing negativity: Sage, pine, and lavender
Protection: Pine, cinnamon sticks, thyme,
and rosemary
Positivity: Sage, rosemary, and sunflower petals
Abundance: Cedar, basil, ginger, cinnamon sticks,
sunflower petals
Love: Cinnamon sticks, rose petals, gardenia
petals, lavender
Psychic awareness / spiritual connection: Sage,
jasmine, thyme, and juniper
Mental clarity: Sage, rosemary, and peppermint

HOW TO MAKE
DRAGON'S BREATH INCENSE
FOR WISDOM

You will need a mortar and pestle, an empty jar
and the following herbs: sage, mint, rosemary
and basil which represent wisdom, clarity,
protection and power. Blend three tablespoons
of each of the herbs and blend to a fine powder
and add the incense. Empower the incense
by saying:

Red Dragon of fiery might
Lend your wisdom, send your light
Celtic drake old and wise
May your breath filter truth from lies
Dragon's breath smoking free
Knowledge is power, so mote it be.

When the raven, Branwen was mistreated
by her husband, the king of Ireland,
her brother Bran extracted revenge in
a great battle. There he rescued his sister,
but was struck by a poisoned dart.
He gave orders that his head was to
be removed and buried at the site
that is now the Tower of London,
where his sacred ravens still reside.

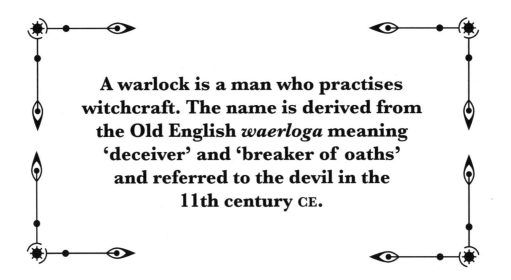

A warlock is a man who practises
witchcraft. The name is derived from
the Old English *waerloga* meaning
'deceiver' and 'breaker of oaths'
and referred to the devil in the
11th century CE.

The legend of the phoenix dates to
ancient times. It was believed that only
one could live in the world at a time.
Every morning, the phoenix sings
a beautiful song to the sun.
And before it dies, it sings a final song
and is then engulfed in flames. Out of the
ashes, a new phoenix arises – and is the
symbol of resurrection and immortality

Cernunnos, the horned one, is the most important of the Celtic deities. A powerful god of forest and animals, he is the guardian of wildlife and wildwood places. He can be turned to for strength, courage, fertility, passion and protection. He can be invoked with this traditional chant:

Hoof and horn, hoof and horn
All that dies shall be reborn
Cernunnos, Horned One
Guide my steps till day is done

SPELL TO KEEP THE HOME PROSPEROUS

Visualize your house as a place of joy and
abundance with images that build on that idea.
At the new moon, take as many dried bay leaves
as you have doors or windows in your home.
Place them on a pentacle to charge and hold your
hands over them as you say:

I charge and bless these leaves of wealth
May they bring financial health

Let the leaves charge until the moon is full,
then anoint each with a dab of patchouli oil.
The place a leaf at every window and door.
Use gold drawing pins to stick them in place,
representing the sun. As you do this, repeat
this chant:

Leaves of wealth, abundance bring
Prosperity makes this happy home sing
Light and warmth, fuel and food
All is bright and all is good
Bless this house with prosperity
By my magic, so shall it be.

Keep the leaves in place for a full year then
repeat the spell with new leaves. Burn the old
ones in a cauldron and give thanks as you do so.

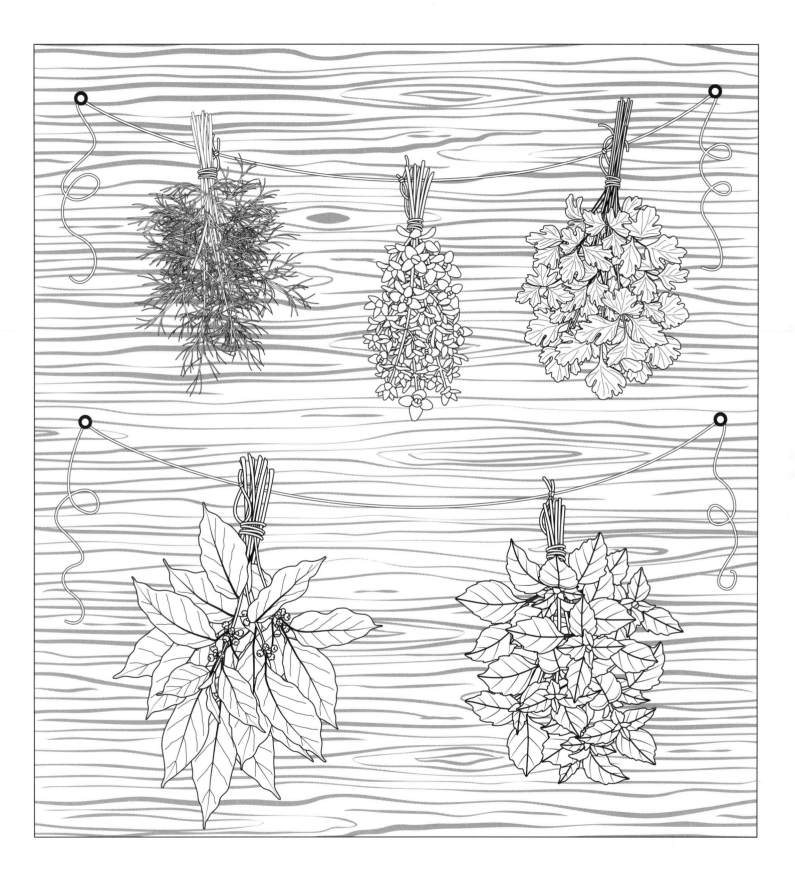

Textbooks of magic were known as *grimoires*. They contained instructions on how to create magical objects like talismans and amulets, how to perform magical spells, charms and divination, and how to summon supernatural entities such as angels, spirits, deities and demons. Often, the books themselves were thought to possess magical powers, Similar books can be found throughout the world.

In Norse mythology, the god Loki has a daughter named Hel or Hela. She is the queen of the afterlife. He mother is the giantess Angrboda and she is sister of Fenrir the wolf and Jörmungandr the World Serpent. Although often referred to as a goddess, Hel is rather a half-goddess and half-jötunn, a giant.

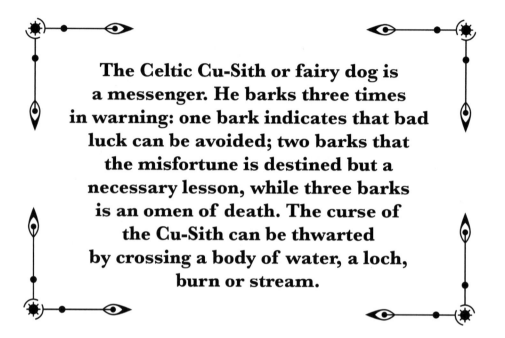

The Celtic Cu-Sith or fairy dog is
a messenger. He barks three times
in warning: one bark indicates that bad
luck can be avoided; two barks that
the misfortune is destined but a
necessary lesson, while three barks
is an omen of death. The curse of
the Cu-Sith can be thwarted
by crossing a body of water, a loch,
burn or stream.

SPELL FOR A YEAR OF BLESSINGS

To make many blessings come your way
throughout the year, take 12 birthday candles
and holders. Place them in the light of the full
moon, then in the rays of the sun at noon.
Put them in a green pouch and hold the pouch
to your heart as you say:

Candles of potential flame
Bring bright blessings in witchcraft's name
A blessing from afar comes near
And keeps me joyful all the year
Blessings beyond all I dare to dream
Are on the way, coming straight to me
As each tiny flame burns so bright
My life is filled with love and light
So mote it

On the first day of every month, light one of
the candles and allow it to burn down, bringing
blessings your way.

BRAVEHEART SPELL
FOR ADVENTURE

If you ever feel trapped or hemmed in, this spell
can help rouse your spirit of adventure.
Take a golden candle and carve the worlds
Braveheart and Adventure down the length.
Light the candle and chant the incantation below
three times, then let the candle burn down.

Razzle, dazzle flying free
The spirit of adventure carries me
From a mundane cage I now depart
I unleash my power as a true braveheart.

Fairy rings of mushrooms or toadstools
were originally associated with the
presence of fairies or elves. According
to some English and Celtic folk tales,
a human who steps into a fairy ring
will have to dance with the creatures
of that ring until they die of exhaustion
or otherwise go mad. Other trespassers
were whisked away to the land
of the fairies, or fell into a
hundred-year sleep.

A modern witch's pantry will be determined by the space you have available but it is here that you can keep your jars of dried herbs and spices, essential oils, spell jars, pouches and candles, incense, smudge bundles and crystals. Keep other tools such as your pentacle, mortar and pester close by so you have everything to hand when needed.

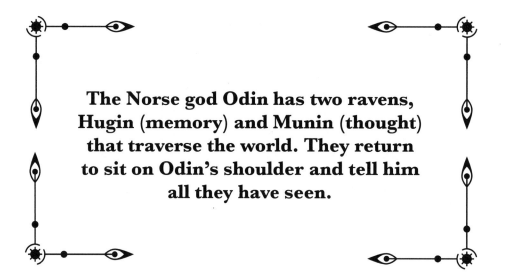

The Norse god Odin has two ravens,
Hugin (memory) and Munin (thought)
that traverse the world. They return
to sit on Odin's shoulder and tell him
all they have seen.